How to Talk * to Moms

BY ALEC GREVEN

ILLUSTRATIONS BY KEI ACEDERA

Collins
An Imprint of HarperCollinsPublishers

Collins is an imprint of HarperCollins Publishers.

How to Talk to Moms
Text copyright © 2009 by Alec Greven
Illustrations copyright © 2009 by Kei Acedera

Printed in the U.S.A.

Library of Congress Cataloging-in-Publication Data
is available.
ISBN 978-0-06-171001-8 (trade bdg.)

Typography by Ray Shappell
1 3 5 7 9 10 8 6 4 2
❖ First Edition

CONTENTS

INTRODUCTION

There are lots of things moms do that bug you.
Such as making you do the laundry.
Who wants to sort your brother's underwear?
Or clean the mess that's in the basement.

But guess what?
Moms also do all sorts of things to help you out.
Moms take care of you and feed you and give you advice.
Being a mom is a really, really hard job because we
don't always follow directions and things can get wild.

Kids do lots of things that bug moms.
You know what I am talking about.
But even when you bug your mom, she still loves you.
That's the best part.

CHAPTER ONE

What's Up with Mom?

{ *Sometimes you think your mom is mean and wants to ruin your life.* }

Sometimes your mom seems like the most wonderful
woman in the world.
But sometimes you think she is mean
and wants to ruin your life.
Really, it is both.

You probably think your mom is wonderful
when she is doing something nice for you, like:
- ✓ Helping you with homework
- ✓ Letting you play all day
- ✓ Reading to you
- ✓ Taking you out to eat

You probably think your mom is trying to ruin your life when she makes you:

- ✓ Clean
- ✓ Rake leaves
- ✓ Go to bed early
- ✓ Eat asparagus

Or if she punishes you by:

✓ Sending you to your room
✓ Taking away your games and toys

The mom job is hard.
If you go to the dark side and cause trouble, she has to be tough.

So moms make your life easy and hard at the same time.
That's just the way it is.

CHAPTER TWO

What Moms Like

*{ When you clean up by yourself without being asked,
you will probably get some big rewards. }*

Moms like nice notes.
When you mess up,
write a note and say you are sorry.

Moms like hugs. Give lots of hugs
and not just to get what you want.

Moms like clean kids.
It will make your mom smile if you
take a shower and comb your hair.
They also like you to wash your hands a lot
and wear clean clothes.

Moms like polite kids. Try to have nice manners.
Use "please" and "thank you" and "may I."
Ask to be excused from the table and wipe your face.

A good way to surprise your mom and make her happy
is to clean up around the house,
like your room, the basement, or the family room.

When you clean up without being asked,
you will probably put Mom in a good mood, and that is great.
You might get some big rewards.

Some types of rewards are:
✓ Taking you to the movies
✓ Letting you stay up late
✓ Letting you have friends over

CHAPTER THREE

What Moms Don't Like

{ *Moms don't like to find weird stuff in your pockets.* }

Moms don't like it when you use your shirt as a napkin or a Kleenex.

Moms don't like to find weird stuff in your pockets.
Make sure to empty them of things
that are alive or sticky or gross.

Moms don't like you to fight with your brother and sister.
They don't like you to whine or yell.

Moms don't like you to do bad pranks,
like tripping your brother or dumping water on him.

Moms don't like loose wildlife in the house.
But who doesn't like to catch things?
And of course if you catch stuff,
you want to keep it for a while.

But remember this important tip:
When you catch bugs, spiders, or snakes
and you want to bring them inside,
make sure you use a container with a lid.
Keep them locked down.

Some moms are easygoing. Some moms freak out a lot.
It helps you if you know what your mom likes and doesn't like.
If you understand your mom, you won't get in trouble as much.

CHAPTER FOUR

How Moms Bug Their Kids

{ *Sometimes it seems like moms are obsessed with cleaning and chores.* }

Most kids don't care about things being clean, but moms do.
Sometimes it seems like moms are obsessed with
cleaning and chores.
Clean your room, clean the basement, clean your face.
Walk the dog. Put the dishes away.
Or the worst—clean the toilet.
All these things bore kids.

You need to be smart when your mom asks you to clean.
If it is a little mess, clean up without hesitation
and she will love it.
This is worth a lot because moms remember the good stuff you do.
Plus, you will probably get a lot of compliments and hugs.

Try to stay low and make little messes
so that your mom doesn't get mad.
If you do make a big mess,
clean it up immediately or your mom will go nuts.
And you will get in serious trouble!

If your mom asks you to clean your little brother's room, add some touches, like putting a rock under his pillow, just to give him a little punishment for having to clean his room.

But sometimes cleaning works out for you.
Every three out of four missing toys are found when
cleaning huge messes!

CHAPTER FIVE

Excuses, Bribes, and the Backfire

{ Moms are smart cookies and they don't like excuses,
so I don't recommend them. }

Kids try and say no to Mom all the time.
You might try to protest or make up an excuse.
But beware of the backfire!
The backfire is when your plan goes very wrong.

When you try to get out of something your mom wants you to do,
95 percent of the time you will get the backfire.

When you don't want to clean,
one way to say no is to try protesting.
Don't give up without a fight.
Here are ways to protest:
- ✓ But, but, but. But I need help.
- ✓ Why can't I do it later?
- ✓ But I am hungry.

TIP: *The backfire happens about 45 percent of the time with Dad,*
and maybe 1 percent of the time with Grandma.
(Everybody knows that grandmas spoil you.)

If you protest, you need to use caution.
You will probably make your mom mad, get in big trouble,
and still have to do that thing you don't want to do.
Backfire!

You could also try to make up an excuse,
like saying your stomach hurts to get out of doing chores.
But your mom will probably make you stay in bed
all day long doing nothing.
Backfire!

Try an excuse if you want,
but don't come crying to me when it doesn't work.
Moms are smart cookies and they don't like excuses,
so I don't recommend them.

Sometimes your mom asks you to do something
and offers you a bribe.
An example of a bribe is when your mom says,
"If you clean up the living room, we can go to the pool."

Maybe you think it isn't worth it
and you don't want to go to the pool *that* bad.
But if your mom asks you to do something and offers a bribe,
you might as well take it.
If you don't, she probably will get mad and make you do it anyway,
and then you don't get the treat.
Backfire!

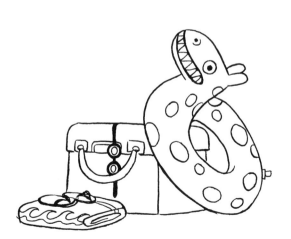

CHAPTER SIX

How Kids Bug Their Moms

{ When you make concoctions with stuff like Mom's perfume or food, you are probably going to get in trouble. }

Kids do a lot of things that bug their moms.
You know the obvious things,
like fighting with your brother and sister and yelling.

But these aren't the only things.
Making stews, potions, and other concoctions is fun
because you mix all sorts of ingredients.
Usually it is best to use natural things
like leaves, grass, rocks, and stuff like that.

When you make concoctions with stuff
like Mom's perfume or food,
you are probably going to make her mad.
No more Miss Nice Mom for sure!

You will also get in trouble if you make a big mess,
use Mom's flowers, or make your concoctions
in Mom's things (like the birdbath or the fountain).

It is a good idea to ask your mom first
and try not to do undercover activities.
Undercover activities are when you don't ask your mom
and you try to hide it.
Moms do not like undercover concoctions.
But the funny part is she probably did it when she was a kid.

CHAPTER SEVEN

Why I Love My Mom

{ *Moms love you no matter what.* }

Moms really don't want to ruin your life.
Moms just want to help you succeed and be better.
They make you do things you don't want to do,
but they do all sorts of things to help you.

Moms read to you and play games with you.
Moms play soccer with you and camp out with you.
Moms fix broken things for you.
Moms drive you everywhere you need to go.
Moms take you on vacation.

Moms take care of you and feed you,
give you advice, help you with your homework,
and help you sort out problems.
Plus they love you no matter what.

Remember what your mom does for you
and what you can do to make her happy.

Even when you bug each other,
you always love each other.
And that's the best part!

ACKNOWLEDGMENTS

For my mom,
of course!